T0247811

THE WAY *of the* CHAMPIONS

Discover the 9 Essential Skills for Career and Life Success

Creator of the Otacílio Gama Institute

OTHAMAR GAMA

The Way of the Champions:
Discover the 9 Essential Skills for Career and Life Success
Othamar Gama

1. Success in business 2. Success 3. Self-help I. Title
Index for systematic catalog:
1. Success in business

Print ISBN: 979-8-35093-944-6
eBook ISBN: 979-8-35093-945-3

I dedicate this book to my father, who inspired me with his examples of solidarity and respect for his fellow men, and to my mother, whose unconditional love and wisdom has guided me in this life.

ACKNOWLEDGMENTS

I have a goal notebook that I always use when the year comes to a close. In this secret notebook, to which I alone have access, I always write my goals for the coming year in various dimensions of my life. At the end of my list of goals, I pray for God's guidance to help me fulfill my goals at the right time, in the right way. For the past few years, I have written "to write a book" as one of my main goals, which I had not yet achieved—until now.

I learned early on in my life that almost nothing can be done without help. What matters most is that what is done, is done with love and the help of other people. This book is no different: it was possible only thanks to the support from many loved ones, including my wife, Ana Raquel, who has helped me from the very first moment of this journey, from initial discussions right to the very end. Her input in the book's design and enthusiasm for my project were extremely fundamental.

I want to thank my daughter Caroline for her support with editing and inputting suggestions to the text—and to highlight her willingness to help at any time during the process.

I want to give a special thank you to my daughter Sophia, who encouraged me to translate this book into English and aided in the process.

Another big thank you goes to my son Othon, who has encouraged me to write this book. With his contagious enthusiasm, he has helped me make this entire project come true.

I also thank my son Othamar Filho, who helped me publish this book in the United States, and Thamara and Thiane for sharing their own life stories, which are great examples of skills I refer to later in this book.

I also consider myself a fortunate man to have a wonderful mother-in-law, Maria José, who helps support our family.

If you want to get to know a person—to truly know them—work with them. Working these past twenty years with the same team at the Otacílio Gama Institute has been a great privilege because I've had the blessing to work alongside people who are committed to a cause and dedicated to making a difference. I want to thank everyone at Gama: Ana, Duda, Renato, Walter Jr., Fernando Ligia, Ivanildo (may he rest in peace), and everyone else who participated in this project. Your work enhances our state of Paraiba. Thank you for all you did and continue to do.

I want to thank Professor Onacir Carneiro Guedes for his encouragement at a pivotal moment in my life.

I also want to thank Aramis, Walter, and all the alumni who have worked with us. Through their stories, they have played a crucial role in contributing to this book, as have the thousands of students who have passed through our institute in the past twenty years and taught us so much.

TABLE OF CONTENTS

FOREWORD

I remember playing in our hometown, João Pessoa, with my father. At seven years old, just like every other healthy child at that age, I loved to play, explore, question, and test boundaries. One day, I noticed a wall that was slightly taller than I was at the time; feeling quite courageous, I decided to climb it.

With extreme difficulty, I managed to climb to the top *and* maintain my balance, celebrating my achievement by walking around with open arms. After rejoicing a little at the crest of my accomplishment, I came down hard and breathless, and celebrated that small conquest with my father. It might have seemed small to the outside world, but to me, it felt as if I had climbed Mount Everest.

As young as I was, I didn't understand the wisdom behind my father's attitude. However, throughout my entire climb of "Mount Everest", my father *willingly* accompanied me every step of the way. Not one time did he scold or discourage me. On the contrary, he supported was supportive, being careful to catch me if I fell. He was like the safety nets trapeze artists use at the circus. In case something went wrong, he was close enough to catch me, but always encouraged me to go further. Not until many years later did I begin to understand how important his encouragement was to my personal growth. My father's encouragement continued throughout my career: not only had he taught me to believe in my dreams; he also helped me develop the personal skills of commitment, persistence, discipline, and dedication that were necessary to see them through. I am honored write this foreword, especially after hearing time and again that it had been my father's dream to publish a book. What child isn't filled with joy as they watch their parents realize their dreams, knowing that they played an active role in their success?

Today, I am a writer, speaker, and mentor who helps high-performance athletes and business executives live to their fullest potential. My books are published in Brazil and across Europe. Throughout my career, I have given lectures to audiences of thousands of people.

I'm writing this foreword because I was always an average child-like others in my class, I wasn't the best in school, sports, or art. Unlike many, however, I had my father's orientation and guidance to help me develop the self-confidence, self-esteem, courage, and optimism I needed to succeed later in life. I can say, with utmost conviction, that his teachings were fundamental to my personal development.

I think it's important to tell you, the reader, that at age twenty-nine, I was able to achieve my biggest dreams because of the skills and practices that this book addresses. This work by Othamar Gama combines two incredible strands of learning that are extremely difficult to intertwine: practical experience and theoretical knowledge. These two components can be supported, taught, and written by Othamar Gama because they are found within him, an entrepreneur with a long list of management experiences. With his studious and passionate ways, he is always seeking to amplify his knowledge and improve his personal development. Othamar shows these two components through his example of life as an educator. He supports the theory that it's possible to help people do good, teach the youth how to become champions in life, and contribute to Brazil's efforts in training more compassionate doctors and healthcare professionals. All these experiences make this narrative truly inspiring. It is not merely meant to be read superficially, but rather to be internalized and cherished in our minds and hearts, always promoting personal growth and positive action.

Even today, when I am faced with the most difficult situations in life, I automatically recall the wisdom that my father teaches to everyone, which has been sprinkled over the stories told in the following pages. Therefore, this book is a must-read for all who wish to not only develop as a person, but to also apply this knowledge in the development of their children, their employees, and their society as a whole. After all, there are a lot of rough diamonds out there: your kids, your employees, and even yourself. Very few specialists, however, know how to polish the brilliance of a precious gemstone. This book has come to be that guiding light.

Othon Gama

Entrepreneur and Writer

PREFACE

I wrote this book with the goal of inspiring people and showing them that we have the power to shape our own destiny and create the future we desire. When I talk about "building," I mean that in order to achieve anything, we need to plan ahead, use the right tools, skills, and work diligently to bring our projects to life. Based on my life experiences, I realized the importance of understanding our personal strengths. That's why I decided to write this book in simple language, providing information that can help anyone who wants to succeed in their career and life.

I will try to answer questions that we ask in our daily lives, such as:

"Why do some people achieve success while others don't?"

"Why are the best students often not the best professionals?"

"Why does life seem more difficult for some than others?"

"Why are does 'fortune' favor some people instead of others".

I have attempted to answer these questions by telling stories and showing that we all possess personal skills that, when developed, can make a huge difference in our lives and careers. Focusing your attention on these skills will make you reflect on them. This will be the first step towards success.

Then, it will be necessary to take action, to work internally to achieve small goals that gradually consolidate changes in fundamental attitudes for embarking on our journey of personal fulfillment.

I recommend this book to people of all ages—from the young, who are looking to choose a profession or direction and to develop their personal skills, to the more experienced, who already have a career but might be looking for a raise in income at work.

With this book, I also want to help those who are looking for their first job and those who wish to improve their personal relationships. I want to help parents who, in the difficult but important task of raising their children, will need to develop and strengthen these skills. And finally, this book is for those who have not yet given up on their dream of success and wholeheartedly believe that change begins in the way we think.

Happy reading!

INTRODUCTION

In Pursuit of Guidance

"I can give you nothing that has not already its origins within yourself. I can throw open no picture gallery but your own. I can help make your own world visible—that is all."

—Herman Hesse, writer.

When I was eleven years old, I experienced the heartbreaking loss of my father. After almost two years of battling throat cancer, he suddenly left us one day. My family, which consisted of my late father, mother, my three siblings, and myself, became incomplete. I lost my anchor in this world, my childhood hero, and my favorite companion for weekend adventures. In my innocent mind, I held onto the belief that my father would recover any moment and return home so we could go fishing on Bessa Beach in Joao Pessoa, Brazil, where we resided.

I thought it wouldn't be long before we gathered cashews and araca fruit from the nearby woods, close to our summer house. I always accompanied him as we worked together at the family-owned magazine distributor. However, all those plans were shattered, and despite the unwavering support of my entire family, I felt an overwhelming sense of loneliness.

My mother, who possessed immense strength and courage, continued to care for me, my siblings, and the household. My brother Tasso, when he wasn't studying for his civil engineering degree, took charge of managing the family business. My sister Nadma assisted Mom at home and worked at our magazine distributor. Even my brother Omar contributed to the distributor's operations. Being the youngest of the four, I enjoyed going to work early, giving me ample time in the afternoon to learn new tasks and skills.

For a span of three years, this became our way of life. I attended school in the mornings and headed to the distributor in the afternoons. My pocket always held some money, allowing me to indulge in snacks, go to the movies, and occasionally satisfy my sweet tooth. Conveniently situated next to our company was the World of Chocolates, and perhaps that proximity contributed to my perpetual battle with weight gain.

I used to socialize with the employees of the distributor and the news stand vendors who sold magazines on the streets. I was friends with the street vendors who set up a shop near our office; I knew everyone around there. I must confess it was a good life, and I found it enjoyable to work.

Sometimes, on Saturday nights, when the truck arrived with the new batch of magazines, my siblings and I would unload them. These magazines would then be distributed on Monday. After we finished and were exhausted from carrying countless packages up and down several floors, we would treat ourselves to a hot dog from one of the street vendors and enjoy some sugarcane juice.

I adopted a profound love for reading, encompassing everything from comic books and picture books to paperback adventures. I consumed every piece of literature that graced our doorstep with enthusiasm. However, a pivotal event shifted the course of existence. Precisely three years post my father's demise, our agreement with the magazine distribution company was suddenly and one-sidedly severed. In an abrupt twist, the following week's magazine deliveries were shifted to our fiercest competitor. This seemingly trivial incident turned our family's livelihood upside down.

Tasso had to sell the family car and start a new business in a field we had never worked in before. He bought an old dump truck that kept breaking down. We went through tough times with serious financial setbacks, but I never heard anyone in my family complain about anything. Each member was busy doing his or her part when we were faced with this crisis. Not only that—they were each doing it with strength and dignity. There was no more money for the movie theater or snacks.

For me, even though I may not have had money, I had a profound passion for judo. This passion propelled me to train diligently every day and soon, I began setting new ambitions: to compete in tournaments and emerge victoriously. By 1976, I was already acquiring recognition as an athlete blossoming with potential. As a result, both the school and the judo academy awarded me a scholarship. This significantly eased our family's financial burden.

At the age of seventeen, a new chapter began in my life. I started teaching judo to the children at my school. To my surprise and delight. I discovered an innate talent for teaching. I found immense satisfaction in guiding children to develop their skills through sports. Moreover, the parents of my students also appreciated my work and frequently attended their children's classes displaying their endearing support.

It was during this time that my first opportunity presented itself. There were scarcely any local markets for judo uniforms, so many parents approached me seeking advice on where to purchase their children's uniforms. I offered to have them custom-made if they were interested. Recognizing a high demand, I hired a seamstress to create the uniforms while I took care of purchasing the fabric. This marked the beginning of earning my own money doing something I loved!

Like many young people who are nearing the age of eighteen, I hadn't yet determined which profession to pursue or what skills were necessary for success in life. Up until that point the only thing I had figured out was my passion for judo and teaching. However, I aspired of going beyond merely instructing. I yearned for a flourishing career, recognition, and substantial wealth.

The problem was: where and with whom to seek help? In school, they only taught the mandatory curriculum subjects: math, Portuguese, physics, chemistry, biology, English, etc. Nothing taught me decision-making or how to become an entrepreneur. What I knew was only useful for entrance exams or to take a middle-level public exam.

My family and I attended church, every Sunday, listening to the priest's sermons, which we held in high regard. Yet, as I listened carefully, I sometimes found it challenging to translate these teachings into practical measures for my daily life. Respectful of these teachings, I was also desiring guidance that would be more specific to pursuing my ambitions to trail my dreams. I felt the need to learn something that would propel me further. While I was content with my life and its current trajectory, I also wanted to improve, pursue greater heights, and embark on new endeavors. However, I didn't know where to begin. My peers seemed to be wandering through life without clear direction, just like me.

Whoever Searches Will Find!

The saying, "whoever searches will find" proved to be true in my life. One day, I was at a judo tournament in Belo Horizonte. I went alone on a day off after the competition and took a walk downtown. I stepped into a bookstore and a title quickly caught my eye: *As a Man Thinketh* by James Allen. This book would soon be on my bedside table, and it would change my life. I opened it up to a random page and what was written there in black and white called to me in such a way that I knew it had to be a sign: "Good thoughts and good deeds cannot produce bad results; evil thoughts and evil deeds cannot produce good results."

It was then that I bought my first self-help book, which I later realized had been a very important diversion in my life. I can say it was a turning point, a very vital crossroad I came across where the road split in two. In practical and simple language, it gave me valuable information about things I had never heard anywhere else. Since then, I have never stopped searching for more knowledge to help me become a more successful person.

Soon thereafter, I found books on positive thinking, which raved about the laws of success and about the power of the subconscious and personal magnetism. Before long, I had a long list of books that helped me see the world in a different light, make my own decisions, and face each difficulty with optimism and courage. In the books, I found the words and guidance I had been looking for my life.

I finished high school, and as I was getting ready for the college admissions test, I decided to launch my first company: a judo academy called Clube Judo Hipopotamo. I came up with the name because the hippo is a heavy animal—stable and hard to bring down.

I needed to find a place to rent but a major obstacle lay ahead. I didn't have enough money. However, the universe conspired in my favor. I didn't know it, but the place I wanted to rent belonged to the principal of the school I had attended my entire life. He trusted and rented it to me without even signing a contract—just by giving me his word.

I spent a year and a half running my first business venture. I was a handyman. I taught classes, answered the phone, was a receptionist, *and* cleaned out the place after sessions—every single day. It was an extremely important experience in my career as an entrepreneur and gave me the opportunity to do some social work.

While I was giving classes on an everyday basis, I noticed two kids—both humble in appearance and nature—were simply watching from the beginning without jumping in. One day, after finishing a class, I asked them if they wanted to learn judo. As quickly as possible, they replied that they did. They didn't have the means to pay for it, however. I didn't need them to tell me they didn't have money—I could tell just by looking at them. Their eyes glittered while watching the students' movements during class, so I made the following proposal: I would provide the uniforms and they would take the classes. In exchange, they had to sweep the gym at the end of the day. Enthusiastically, they accepted my proposal without a second thought.

When I looked at the boys, I felt overjoyed. I had just given them an opportunity to help them achieve their dreams, have hope for their future, and become high-level athletes. It was like unlocking a door for them.

We reap what we sow, don't we? Recently, I was interviewed for a TV channel. At the end of the interview, when the cameras were off, the cameraman came up to me and thanked me for the opportunity I had given him—not the opportunity to film me for the interview, but the one I gave him when he was just a child in a judo class. He said the gesture changed his life and his friend from that time in his childhood also turned into a successful and accomplished professional. You can't imagine the wonderful sensation that came over me. At that moment, I recognized the importance of that small task of social responsibility.

I decided to close the gym once I passed the civil engineering entrance exam. That same year, I also passed the test to be an officer in an army reserve. It was a huge learning period and more than ever before, I needed the teachings of those books from when I was seventeen to rise to the challenges I was taking on, day in and day out.

I still wonder how many millions of young people are in the same situation I was in, with access to only theoretical knowledge and without any information about how to apply it in a practical way. Little is said about the importance of personal development, which can be the dividing line between success and failure. It's important to say *no* school teaches these crucial skills that are cause for us to become champions in life.

For those who have difficulty in finding where best to look for help in learning about these personal skills, even our schools today barely offer pedagogical practices that stimulate students in ways that are genuinely helpful in life. They don't stimulate students in integral ways, offering self-sustenance and contributing to their development into successful, happy, and accomplished professionals who can say they "won" in life. While the job market looks for those with fundamental skills and knowledge, our archaic system merely teaches us solid facts; they do not emphasize the significance of developing principles that differentiate us from other employees.

We need to work internally to grow the seeds we've sown through essential skills like goodwill and perseverance, optimism, and courage. We need to have the will to win without being afraid of obstacles. I'm not saying we should shy away from external aid or scientific knowledge. What I mean is this: if we do not prepare ourselves internally, getting to know our personal skills and developing them, we will never see the opportunities in front of us.

I've learned over the years that there are no insurmountable obstacles. The help we need to get over them can come through books, lectures, movies, advice, or organizations that give us this knowledge. What's important is that it touches our soul, makes us reflect, and helps us make better decisions.

We can't let misinformation guide our thinking. When we are amid our day-to-day tasks, we usually don't have time to form our own thoughts—instead, we easily adhere to others' mindsets, getting their desires and their fears. We keep moving on like this without moving forward, without knowing where we want to go. On the other hand, we *must* know where we want to go with our lives. The Internet, social networks, television, radio, and other media outlets begin to take more control of our thoughts and ways of living than we would like. They recreate our wants and stir misguided beliefs within us, challenging our inner beliefs about how far we can go or what we can be. And that's something I never let happen!

"I just gave them an opportunity to help themselves achieve their dreams, have hope in their future, and become high-level athletes. It was like opening a door for them."

With only two months left before I completed my degree in civil engineering, I was twenty-three and interning at one of the largest construction companies in Brazil. I had my second business, a small cement trade, which wasn't doing so well. But that didn't stop me from keeping my dreams and goals high. I wanted to be a respected businessman.

One day, after I had completed a year of training, the head engineer responsible for the project on which I was working called me to his office. He had great news: I would be hired as an engineer as soon as I graduated.

Of course, I was happy with the compliments and recognition from my boss, who had extensive experience in the market. He could never have predicted my response, however. My answer took him completely by surprise. I thanked him for the offer and said I wanted to have my own company. Already aware of my financial difficulties, he said I should think about it; I was throwing away a great opportunity and it wasn't easy to get a job like the one on the table.

Making the decision at that moment wasn't easy. I already had a one-year-old son to raise and no one to help me keep him. The decision took courage and more than that—a belief in my dreams. It was a turning point in my future as an entrepreneur.

Years later, as a successful businessman, I made the decision to establish a nonprofit institute dedicated to assisting at-risk children.

My goal was to share the knowledge I had gained to succeed in life, something that may not be taught in schools. I firmly believed that through sports, I could help these children develop essential qualities such as self-confidence, perseverance, teamwork, and discipline. Thus, I named this project the "Factory of Winners."

To pay tribute to my father, I founded the Otacílio Gama Institute, a nonprofit organization that has now been in operation for twenty-six years. Throughout this time, it has positively transformed the lives of at-risk children by engaging them in sports and cultural activities. Utilizing positive psychology concepts, we foster the development of skills necessary for personal triumph.

As a child, I vividly recall observing my father extending opportunities to street kids to sell magazines through our distribution business. This endeavor provided them with a head start in life, similar to how he had begun by selling newspapers. My father, with immense patience, not only offered them guidance but also shared his own story, inspiring and encouraging those boys. That simple act of support significantly altered the trajectory of their lives, and I can affirm that many of them achieved success due to that small gesture of encouragement.

"We must cultivate internal growth, nurturing the seeds we've sown, employing fundamental skills such as goodwill, perseverance, optimism, and courage. We should possess the determination to succeed without fear of obstacles."

Motivated by the desire to emulate the examples set by my father, I launched various initiatives at the Otacílio Gama Institute. My aim was to immortalize not just his name but also his acts of kindness and inspiration.

Through this book, my intention is to demonstrate that certain skills can be developed and nurtured in our minds, enabling us to lead fulfilled lives with significant goals that help us achieve our dreams. By incorporating one or more of those skills discussed here into your life while reading this book, you will equip yourself with powerful tools necessary to make decisions that align with your personal success and prosperity, enabling you to become a champion in life.

1 WE CAN CHOOSE OUR THOUGHTS

"Our life is what our thoughts make it."

—Emperor Marcus Aurelius

Imagine you're going to prepare a meal for you and your family. You get your pan and begin putting together ingredients, choosing horrible-quality products of bitter and sour taste—those that are spoiled and rotten.

Then you invite your loved ones to eat the meal you just prepared. Day after day, you continue doing the same: preparing poor-quality meals and then serving them.

What could you expect would come out of this? Surely everyone will get sick! We can say: "This is absurd! No one would do such a thing." Unfortunately, we do this every day with our thoughts. We put the worst ingredients in our minds—fear, envy, despair, distrust, anger—then offer them up on a plate of emotions. The truth is that we have an obligation to be selective with the thoughts we place in our minds. We shouldn't keep our focus on news that will intoxicate our spirit and poison our emotions. We have the ability to choose where to direct our attention.

What Are Our Priorities?

We can't see radio, television, or Wi-Fi waves, but we know they're there and that we need the correct equipment to tune each one of them. Just like these devices of technological communication, our mind has the ability to tune waves of thought that circulate in the environment. In automatic mode, we get in tune with the thoughts we produce. Therefore, we need to be very careful with the types of thoughts we let into our mind because from there, we attract people, events, and other parts of our day to our lives.

Taking care of our thoughts is just as important as the health of our physical body. We can set daily goals to put positive thoughts in our minds. Just like a bank account, at the end of the day, we hope (and should) have a positive balance in our savings. In the beginning, this sort of practice takes a lot of effort. However, the salary of our own account will turn into something valuable, helping construct our personal success.

What should we do to avoid the accumulation of negative thoughts? First, we should recognize that we have the power to change the way we think—and this change is entirely up to us. Our positive, healthy thoughts are remedies for the negativity that can invade our minds like a sickness and start us off on a deficit on the way to our dreams.

If there is something that we should always be vigilant about— it's the quality of our mental, social, and physical life. If there's a part of that that you're not doing well with, you should reflect on your own self to help you realize what you need to change. It's no use putting the blame on others—on family, friends, your boss, work, or whatever it may be. There is just one person who can change the world and your surroundings: you.

How? Change how you react to everything that happens. How can you do this?

"We put the worst ingredients in our minds—fear, envy, despair, distrust, anger—then offer them up on a plate of emotions."

Before you begin questioning your reactions, you need to understand the decision-making power you have and how it is divided—between reason and emotion—and how one always influences the other.

We need to think before we act; notice if your reaction agrees with your objective or your positive expectation. Why do we tend to blow up in certain situations? What is our objective when we speak higher or lower to something? Is the expectation behind our reaction trying to protect us? Do you believe it is possible to have both working in cooperation with one another? Only with this quick observation can we have the possibility of change.

The truth is that we normally don't have a lot of time to look inside of ourselves. During the majority of our days, we are involved in decision-making—from the most simple choices to the most complex. Cultivating a bad mood, being rude to people, being arrogant, drinking to excess, always being late to commitments, and engaging in destructive criticism are all examples of everyday decisions that can make a big difference in people's lives. These simple decisions—like to smile, greet people, listen, help, think positive thoughts and hold positive attitudes—can have a major impact on your life. We need to understand that we are very influenced by what or who gives us attention, by the information we seek, by colleagues we are in touch with, by the environments we are in, and by the types of thoughts we let into our mind. Let me tell you a story that I believe can help clarify the point I'm trying to get across.

I had a dog named Kika. When I got home from work, she was always waiting for me at the gate, extremely happy, with her tail wagging freely. As soon as I approached her, she would always jump on me. One day, I got home at the same time I normally do; however, I thought it strange that she wasn't there to greet me—she didn't even move from her spot on the floor. Kika just looked at me and was very sad. I asked those who were at home if something had happened or if she was sick, but nobody knew how to respond.

The next day, really early in the morning, I went for a walk in our garden and I noticed some changes. The gardener had brought some cattle manure to fertilize the plants, and this type of fertilizer often comes with tick larvae and other insect disease transmitters. Quickly, I made the connection to the fertilizer and what had happened to Kika the day before. I ran my hand through her fur and saw it was infested with ticks that were hurting her and sucking away her energy and fun-loving nature. Wasting no time, I called the vet, told him what happened, and asked him to come and examine her as fast as possible.

A few days after being treated with the right medicine, Kika went back to being her playful, happy, and fun self. Why did I tell you this story? Because, just like ticks, negative thoughts can stick onto our minds and suck away our joy, energy, courage, and personality, so we should always be alert and attentive to what comes in our heads. We should be prepared to face threats like negative thoughts, which hover around us, no matter where we are. Negative thoughts come from all sides, affect our emotional state, and come through negative information. To not succumb to the tick of a bad thought, we need allies in this daily fight—especially if we want to head toward success in personal development.

How to Destroy Negative Thoughts

We are responsible for our inner strength. Sometimes, we have to shield ourselves from bad thoughts and bad feelings. We also cannot allow ourselves to be ensnared by a vicious circle that we call unfortunate events. The truth is that we all have—and can use—a powerful tool to help in the arduous task of fighting negative thoughts: our imagination!

For this, we need to create a strong character within us who will be our guardian. His or her job will be solely to mercilessly destroy the negative thoughts. Choose a name for your warrior. Think of all the characteristics your guardian needs to have. Are they fearless, self-confident, optimistic, bold? Choose a color for their armor—preferably your favorite color, which can give you a sense of comfort and security.

After selecting your guardian, it's time to select the most efficient weapon to shoot down those mental enemies. It could be a magical sword with a gold-plated blade of optimism or a magical pistol with silver bullets of faith or even a magical bow with arrows of fire and courage.

Now you have fully created your guardian in your imagination, all you need to do is enable him or her to defend your mind from the constant attacks of your biggest enemies: your negative thoughts. Let's imagine that the negative thoughts are like party balloons. They always come in large quantities, but can pop ever so easily. Don't resist the destructive power your guardian's weapon holds. The faster you can pop them, the better. Although they pop easily, don't be fooled because many others are floating around, always ready to approach. That's why we should always be with our guardian on alert. If we get distracted, lose control of them, we can get so overwhelmed by all the balloons that we have no idea where to begin popping them.

Negative thoughts are always hanging around. The fact is, because of them, we sacrifice the present for a negative expectation of the future—although we have everything we need to be happy, we don't feel that way because we're afraid of what may happen over there or at a future date. We are always waiting for the perfect moment to be happy, but negative thoughts won't ever allow that to happen.

What is the remedy for this evil? We need to think positive thoughts and regardless of our current situation, we need to believe that the future will be much better than where we are. This attitude can help make you feel good, even in difficult situations. Believing in success helps you step firmly into today with the certainty of where you're going: a place of possibilities and achievement. Even in the severest of winters, if we believe that spring will come and with it our positive expectations, this will become our reality.

"The truth is that we all have—and can use—a powerful tool to help in the arduous task of fighting negative thoughts: our imagination!"

2 MAKING DECISIONS

"If you are working on something exciting that you really care about, you don't have to be pushed. The vision pulls you."

—Steve Jobs, inventor

Some time ago, I was with my family, walking in New York. On our schedule that day was a visit to the Metropolitan Museum of Art. I sat in a chair near the reception desk of the hotel, opened the Uber app, and plugged in the address of where we wanted to go. In a few seconds, the information appeared of a car that would pick us up in two minutes. As if by magic, just twenty-five minutes later, we were at the museum.

Although it seems very simple and commonplace nowadays, there is a very explicit detail that made it all happen: everything went smoothly because I knew where we wanted to go. We, as a family, had made the decision to visit the museum and we knew the address— we just didn't know how to actually get there. Life is just about the same way: at first, all we need to know is our destination. Without this knowledge, we won't go anywhere.

The evil of today is that many people don't have a sense of direction in life. They're simply waiting on the decisions of others to move, and they don't know how to move today if they don't know what they want tomorrow. We have to be aware that at this very moment, each of us is building our own future.

Take care of your thoughts. They will be the key to making decisions. We can't forget that decisions bring change into our lives. And change is one of the most important words for our interior reconstruction. Without even realizing it, we move every single day. Our body is also always changing, transforming. Our cells are always attentive to the way we live and will adapt according to how we are going about our day-to-day lives. If we're doing the recommended physical exercise, for example, our muscles will adapt and grow, our cardiorespiratory system will probably improve, and depending on our diet, we can change our fatty cells and increase our lean body mass. If we are taking in alcoholic beverages every day, we know what the cost will be to our physical and mental health. If we choose friends who have different values than us, this will also affect us. As easy as some of these decisions are, each of them always brings change—pleasant or unpleasant, wanted or not.

Change is the only certainty. It's up to us to decide whether it's for the best or not. The good news is that any kind of change happens slowly and gradually, so we always have the time to reverse decisions that are not good for us. Just pay attention to yourself in your life, have sincere conversations with your inner self, and don't try to deceive yourself to see the signs that tell us if we're on the right direction or not: these are the paths that lead to success or the well-being of fullness.

To sabotage ourselves, to try to cheat ourselves, to create a character who doesn't fit us but appeals to those around us is one of the deadliest attacks we can commit against ourselves. It is extremely important to find out—as soon as possible—who that person is who lives within ourselves and learn to like him or her as they are. No one holds prejudice more than the person who doesn't have self-love. As I heard in a lecture from my friend Augusto Cury, a famous Brazilian writer, "We need to have a love affair with ourselves." And this love affair, I guarantee, exists only if we make the decision to improve what we do well and do an analysis on the habits that hinder our personal development.

"We can't forget that decisions lead to change in our life. And change is one of the most important words for our interior reconstruction."

The Path of Success

If we want to walk on the path of success, we need to be aware of the three basic pillars of support for personal success:

- Family and Social Relationships
- Career and Personal Development
- Physical, Mental, and Spiritual Health

It's important to evaluate the decisions we've made in the past and see if they have brought us to where we should be today—and where we want to be. If you are satisfied with your result of the three pillars, this means you have made the right decisions. Are you okay with your family? Do you know how to choose your friends wisely? How is your career going? Are you prepared for new challenges? And your health? Is everything well? Do you have a healthy diet? Are you still smoking? Do you still have that drinking problem? Have you set aside some time to talk to God?

It's one hundred percent necessary to do a reflection and an assessment with full honesty and sincerity about all aspects of your life in reference to these three pillars. For that, try to imagine seeing yourself from the outside, like a spectator watching your routine. Once you've done this, we can start working on your decision-making process.

Remember that decisions made now will have a decisive impact on your life and destiny. To understand that, a great exercise is to make a personal projection for the future. In the next five years, you want to earn a certain amount—but by doing what? If you know how much you want to earn and what you want to do, know you will have to pay a certain price for it. To achieve this, you probably should look into specialized training to set yourself apart from other professionals. If you want to have a successful career, you can't just expect things to fall from the sky. Be optimistic but proactive. Only you can make your dreams come true. Choose your path, don't lose your faith, stay motivated, and focus on what you want to happen.

3 THE ABILITIES OF CHAMPIONS

*"In the battles of life, the first step to victory
is the desire to win."*

—Mahatma Gandhi, peace activist

Everyone likes to watch a champion when he or she is doing their job. Who doesn't admire the ability and skill of an Olympic athlete? Who doesn't admire a good speaker in front of an audience? Who isn't inspired by a story filled with the resilience and success of an entrepreneur?

Everyone agrees winners are naturally admired for their results. However, what's behind these results? There are no magical abilities only the privileged few can have, no genetic inheritance of another civilization or another planet. Champions are normal people—like you and me—who have developed skills that are available to everyone. They are qualities within each one of us. We just need to discover them, work on them, and place them in harmony with our lifestyle and beliefs.

For the past twenty years, at least once a year, I have told the kids at the Otacílio Gama Institute a simple story about the potential and development of their skills. The story I tell is a simple one, but it awakens a habit of reflection and understanding of choices in each of the children—for now and in the future. So here's the story:

One day, a man was walking on the beach when he saw a shiny pebble semi-covered in the sand. He stopped, took the pebble, and held it while he continued to walk. After a few minutes, he let it fall back onto the sand. Soon after, along the same path, walked an older man who was a specialist in precious stones and gems. He saw the pebble that man threw away and picked it up. He stopped immediately, hardly believing what he was seeing with his very own eyes—a diamond in the rough! At that instant, he placed the pebble in his pocket, and as soon as he arrived back at home, he started to polish the pebble. It began to transform. Finally, after the last bit of polishing, the stone acquired an impressive shine. It was definitely worth a lot of money.

"They are qualities within each one of us. We just need to discover them, work on them, and place them in harmony with our lifestyle and beliefs."

To each child I tell this story, I also tell them they're a diamond in the rough. Within them lies immense potential that just needs to be polished so the world can see the true shine underneath. They just need to find out what makes them so special. Just as the pebble hid the precious diamond, a winner's skills are already inside the mind of every single one of us. We just need to awaken them.

In this chapter, we are going to get to know what these skills are and which are important for those who want to win in life. In the next chapters, we are going to dive into each skill and begin to look through the various ways to meet them, develop them, and use them in our favor. This is how we start our search—inside, without hastiness, but with determination. We cannot evolve internally without discovering our strengths and weaknesses.

The Nine Champions' Skills

GOODWILL: An ability of fundamental importance to be able to produce positive results in your professional career. A goodwill can give the power to transform people, making them indispensable wherever they may be—in the workplace, in society, in the community, in the family, etc.

COURAGE: The development of this skill can help you transform into the hero of your own story, which surely will be a success.

PERSISTENCE: This determinant skill is used to set apart those who define a goal and see it through to the end from those who set a goal and never achieve it.

OPTIMISM: A fundamental skill to nourish our dreams and give us the fuel we need to turn them into a reality.

FAITH: This skill allows us to turn what seemed impossible, possible. It can be the biggest difference in achieving a life full of success and an awareness of our connection with God.

RESILIENCE: A skill that allows the champion to adapt and follow in pursuit of their dreams, in spite of all the difficulties that may arise during the journey.

SELF-ESTEEM: The ability to strengthen a social and effective relationship. The starting point for "to love thy neighbor is to love thyself."

SELF-CONFIDENCE: The ability essential to accomplish anything that relies on trust. Self-confidence is the basis for building a healthy character, overcoming a lifetime of challenges and obstacles, and pursuing a path to reliable success.

SOLIDARITY: This is the ability to do good in the world. It is one of the most important skills to have when looking to achieve a life full of accomplishments.

When we help people, we awaken forces—powerful ones—that act on our behalf to strengthen our spirit and increase our inner peace. Doing good is good! In the next chapters, we are going to address each of these skills in detail and explain how they will make a difference in your life.

4 THE POWER OF GOODWILL

"Nothing can possibly be conceived in the world, or even out of it, which can be called good, without qualification, except goodwill."

— Immanuel Kant, philosophy.

Goodwill, what is it? I will try to explain. Throughout my life as an entrepreneur, I have employed thousands of people and, through experience, I have been able to observe what sets some of them apart in terms of their work capacity and interpersonal skills. They carry out their tasks with more dedication, always strive to do their best, focus on execution and the quality of their work, enjoy being helpful, and seek to learn and improve themselves.

Regardless of the situation, these individuals are always available to help, enjoy what they do, and become indispensable wherever they are.

People who work with goodwill are always in a good mood and willing to do more than what is necessary. They are initially a wildcard in any team and later become a leaders committed to results. It's no wonder that there are passages in the Bible that refer to men of goodwill. You might be wondering: is there a way to acquire goodwill? The answer is yes!

It is important to understand that in order to reap any fruit in our minds, we must first plant the right seeds, water them with discipline, and only then harvest the fruit.

As I wrote in the previous chapter, thoughts are precursors to action . We can start an internal process to align our minds with actions that demonstrate people's goodwill and greatness of attitudes that contribute to the growth of the environment we are in. Listening to others is an act of goodwill, as well as helping a colleague without expecting gratitude, and having a willingness to serve…whatever our work may be, there is no task that cannot be improved with the goodwill of the pern preforming it.

There's a story about a boy that I always tell people as an example of goodwill and dedication. Aramis was just like any other child, living in a poor community. At the age of 7, he enrolled in the Otacílio Gama Institute and started playing indoor soccer. Soon, he fell in love with the sport and dedicated himself to it wholeheartedly. For many years, he consistently attended training sessions and always offered to help store the balls and other equipment. Through these small acts, he earned the sympathy of everyone there.

Sometime later, as the President of FCM (Medical University), I recognized the need to establish a program aimed at training children from the Institute for employment. I gathered the teachers and explained that each sports discipline could select two teenagers to participate in internships at FCM, a renowned medical university. The primary objective was to provide these children with an opportunity to gain practical experience across various departments within the institution, wherein their individual competencies and work skills would be observed and assessed. Exceptional candidates would even have the prospect of securing permanent positions. Consequently, they would have the chance to rotate through departments such as the library, finance, human resources, accounting, IT, reprographics, reception, general secretariat, and more.

Once I requested the names to initiate the internship program, Aramis was the first one nominated by coach Ana and other coachers. Since the beginning of the internship, I have received feedback about his willingness to perform tasks, his persistence, and his eagerness to learn new things. When he reached the IT department, his supervisor requested that the management keep him there. Although his technical knowledge was limited, his desire to learn was inversely proportional. After the internship period ended, Aramis became an employee of FCM and continuously demonstrated aptitude for the work, earning the trust of everyone.

Always eager to further develop his profession, we decided to invest in a training project. First, we invested in a technical course in IT, and he excelled in it. Later, we supported him in obtaining a college degree, which he completed with dedication and excellence.

Throughout this journey, Aramis's goodwill and commitment to his work never wavered. He is now a successful professional, a role model for others, and a testament to the power of goodwill and dedication.

Pay Attention to Good Deeds during Your Day

Before you go to bed at night, take a moment to reflect on your day and the actions that have had the most impact. If you wish, write them down in a reflection notebook.

Ask yourself the following questions:

- During which moments did you exhibit goodwill? And during which moments did you not?

- How did those moments impact the course of your day, positively or negatively?

- Have you made yourself available to help those around you?

- What changes could you make to create a more collaborative environment that stimulates the growth and emergence of positive challenges?

Strive to be useful anywhere you may be. Don't expect to be immediately recognized, but either—simply do your part.

5 COURAGE: THE SECRET OF THE CHAMPIONS.

"A true man measures his strength when faced with obstacles."

Antoine de Saint-Exupéry, aviator and writer

Courage is a quality that everyone admires, which makes our eyes shine. When we watch a movie and see our hero risk their life to save or help others, we immediately connect with them. As the movie unfolds and the danger increases, our involvement and support for the character also grow.

There are characters who inspire us with their courage to face dangerous situations, even without having superpowers and being vulnerable like any human. These characters are even more beloved because we identify with them and project our own desires and fears onto them.

We can recall the worldwide successful movie "The Hunger Games," in which the heroine Katniss volunteers to take her younger sister's place in a brutal competition where survival seemed almost impossible. I am certain that anyone who watched the movie or read the book formed an empathetic bond with the character, and as the adventure unfolded, the excitement and support for her overcoming the challenges only grew.

Now leaving fiction and entering real life, we have all had opportunities to demonstrate courage at some point. Maybe not necessarily risking our lives, but facing challenges that our every-day life presents at work, within our families, or in seemingly ordinary situations that require the courage to say yes, say no, or choose something that could radically alter our lives.

Making decisions also requires courage to confront our weaknesses. We tend to be very demanding of ourselves, making it difficult to liberate our spontaneity. We fear judgment from others, we fear disappointing someone else or ourselves. We place a tremendous amount of pressure on our shoulders, and this limits the space that courage has within us.

A very common example is the fear of public speaking. We know extremely capable individuals who become silent in front of a microphone and pale in front of a camera. I myself felt insecure when I had to express myself in public and had to work hard to overcome this fear. Until when will we allow fear to be stronger than our courage? What are we missing out on and losing by preventing courage from guiding us in challenging moments?

I consider sports to be one of the most effective ways to help develop courage. When an athlete is about to participate in a competition and steps onto a court, field, pool, or any chosen space according to their sport, it is common to feel intimidated by the gaze of the spectators. In that moment, there is no turning back. There is only one way out: to face the butterflies in the stomach, present oneself to the audience, and be prepared for the final score. I speak from personal experience.

When I was 14 years old, I participated in my first judo competition. It wasn't easy to overcome the insecurity and fear of losing. When I was called to enter the competition area, it felt like I was carrying twice my weight. My mind went blank, I couldn't remember anything, I felt like an amateur being called to fight. The only thing I knew was that I couldn't give up. I had to fight.

Years later, as a black belt with plenty of experience and many defeats and victories, I wanted to share this same experience with the children of the Otacílio Gama Institute. I could observe how the opportunity to participate in competitions would make a difference in those children's lives. That's where they would start building the courage to confront the unknown, whatever it may be. They would come to realize that those who could conquer fear more swiftly would be able to embrace life's challenging moments and achieve success.

I was able to follow through with the kids for many years, until they became adults. I saw, for the most part, that courage played a defining role in their lives and professional careers. Our project called "Winner Factory" was finally reaping the fruits of all those years of work! Some of these kids became Brazilian and pan-American judo and wrestling winners, while others joined soccer teams in different states. Nevertheless, they all left the Institute with highly developed qualities of champions, which would last throughout for their entire life.

The courage we need to grow within ourselves can find strength even in the small and constant. These small battles help create the well-equipped attitudes we need to fight internal enemies designed to increase fear. For example, we need the courage to get over any embarrassment we may feel when we worry about what people will think of us and how they'll react to what we say and do. There are plenty of times in our lives when we don't do something important to us because of fear of failure, ridicule, or criticism. What's the answer? Give up looking for success because of others? Letting go of your dreams? Expect people to recognize you and thank you without doing anything? No, it can't be like that.

Even if things don't go as expected on the first try, courage compels us to give it another shot. Ultimately, learning how to accept defeat also teaches us how to achieve victory, as both are crucial for success. It is our responsibility, our right, and our privilege to step onto the field and participate.

We have a duty to step onto the field and start playing. You must use your courage to dare to be better, more creative, and more productive. How can you do that?

First and foremost, we need to set being courageous as a goal and choose a strategy to achieve it. That means identifying situations that tend to undermine your courage. What recurring thoughts weaken your belief in overcoming challenges? In moments of adversity, what thoughts should dominate your mind? What mantras should you repeat to yourself daily? Since this will be purely mental work, it is necessary to engage your emotions and imagination to create a clear picture of what you desire in your family life, work or study environment, and social relationships.

"The courage we need to grow within ourselves can find strength even in the small and constant. These small battles help create the well-equipped attitudes to fight internal enemies designed to increase fear."

Remember: we can only live one day at a time, we can only live in the present. Let's dare a little more just for today, set small courage goals for today, decide on small things without worrying about what others will think, just for today. Therefore, let's not be afraid to speak our minds, knowing that not everyone will agree with us. To be happy, we don't need to be universally liked. We need to be polite and respectful while being true to ourselves. Don't be afraid of making mistakes; it is part of our growth. Adopt the motto: "Dare to do something that scares you today. All fear is cowardly and always flees when courage emerges."

Cultivating courage within yourself will be instrumental in determining how far you want to go. Let me provide you with a simple example:

Imagine that you are in a large room with no doors. Surrounding you are several unprotected ladders. Everyone in that room is compelled to climb those ladders. So, you start climbing one, and immediately another, even taller ladder appears. You have the option to descend at that level through the newly appeared door or continue climbing to a higher level. When you reach the second level, you encounter yet another even higher ladder.

You begin to notice that you are getting farther and farther from the ground, and a sense of insecurity starts creeping in. After all, you have climbed quite a bit, but the ladders just keep appearing. You have to make a decision: how far do you want to climb? How far do you want to go?

Certainly, many people will stop at the first ladder, but others will strive to go further. Your courage will determine how far you will go. Try to be braver, don't settle for the first ladder. Those who stop at the first ladder will never have access to the view that can only be enjoyed after overcoming the challenge of height. You don't have to rush to climb. Take a moment on the step that makes you feel insecure, take a deep breath, and then continue climbing slowly, step by step. Keep climbing and dare to take the next step at your own comfortable pace. This is how we gain self-confidence, how we believe in our abilities. Courage needs to be nurtured to grow stronger. Face your fears and climb as high as you desire. Let only yourself decide what you want for yourself. Don't give up on your dreams, believe that you can reach higher heights.

Just a few days after finishing this book, I received an email from Walter Jr. He told me, extremely happily, that he had just been chosen as the Brazilian national coach of wrestling who would be going to the School World Games in early May 2018, in Marrakech, Morocco. He shared that his selection was due to the outstanding performance of six of his students from Otacílio Gama Institute, who were chosen to represent Paraíba in the Brazilian Wrestling Championships and won gold medals. Furthermore, he mentioned that our state, Paraiba, emerged as the overall winner of the entire tournament.

As soon as I got the email, I called Walter Jr. to congratulate him on his great achievement. Besides São Paulo, no other Brazilian state had ever achieved such a result. He thanked me and spoke to me as if it was actually a win of my own. I countered that. "Walter, you got this because of your own effort and persistence, as well as your courage to go for your dreams."

Walter Jr. grew up in extreme poverty in the community close to Bairro do Padre Zé in the city of João Pessoa in Paraíba. When he was twelve, his grandfather, who raised him, enrolled him at the Otacílio Gama Institute to train in judo and soccer. Walter trained almost every single day. When he wasn't at school, he was at the

Institute. After a few months, Walter chose to continue judo, the sport that helped him develop courage.

During every fight, he had to face his own insecurity and find his courage to go against his opponents: he always had a goal in mind, a tournament to win. He knew only through his own effort and persistence could he improve in his technical skills. Thanks to his dedication, he became a judo champion. However, he wanted more.

At twenty years old, he started wrestling, standing out almost immediately. Today, Walter has his degree in physical therapy and is an Olympic wrestling coach in Paraíba. And now he is a Brazilian national team coach as well as an international referee. At thirty-one, Walter might have many dreams he still can chase, but he is a champion and an example for all the youth of Brazil.

Courage needs to be developed the same way we begin a long walk. Regardless of how long the walk is, we need to take the first step and then continue, slowly, until we reach our goal. The first step is the recognition that we need to have courage to win in life, that this skill we admire in others is also inside of us and is imperative to our journey.

Don't forget that, like everything else in life, courage starts small and needs to be used to grow. In the beginning, it can be used in small and simple activities; then, over time, it develops and gets stronger. Only then can we start to use this quality every day, incorporating it in our actions whenever we need to get out of our comfort zone and advance into the unknown. Any change in our lives takes courage if we want to reach new heights. Don't give up if you're trying to be brave. The world respects and admires those who have courage.

6 THE POWER OF PERSISTENCE: BUILDING BLOCK FOR SUCCESS

"All the graces of mind and heart escape when the purpose is not firm."

—William Shakespeare.

Do you know anyone who won in life without being persistent? I don't! We're going to face challenges and difficulties of every kind throughout our life. This is not a pessimistic thought—far from it. It is a realistic statement so that we can prepare ourselves for every moment of our journey.

While I was thinking about how to start writing this chapter about persistence, I remembered one moment when I was watching my granddaughters begin to walk—what a lovely scene! I saw those two babies trying to stay balanced after taking their first step, day after day, standing up, falling down, and trying again with a smile on their face. I said to myself that we can get what we want only through persistence!

This is a fundamental skill you need to develop in order to learn any other skill in life. A child comes into the world already with this quality—but over time, in some cases, we lose the sense of using the skill, whether it's because of convenience, laziness, or too much protection.

No one who has watched a final round at the Olympics and seen an athlete step up on the podium can imagine what's behind that medal. It is the culmination of years of hard work, persistence, a lifetime of dedication, and an unconditional love for the sport. Those who see a successful business can't imagine the difficulties it had to go through, the pressures it had to face, and, on top of all that, the persistence it had to have to take care of the day-to-day tasks. Likewise, when we see a professional, whether it's a doctor, engineer, accountant, or someone who works, takes care of the kids and still looks after the house, all of them need to be persistent in order to take care of their daily tasks.

What do all of these people I just mentioned have in common? None of them gave up on their goals. When building a successful personality, we place different bricks that represent important characteristics, but the mortar that keeps all the bricks together is persistence. This is a fundamental quality that doesn't let us give up on our dreams and that feeds our willpower. Persistence always goes hand in hand with passion. When we fall in love with what we do, everything becomes easier.

Let me tell you what happened to me that helped me a lot when overcoming my life's obstacles. When I was thirteen years old, I wanted to be an athlete—it didn't matter which sport. I tried indoor soccer at first, but my ball skills were terrible. The PE teacher always put me on the bench—even at practice—and I watched my teammates play. After a little while, I decided to try basketball, but I had no coordination to throw the ball properly and was horrible when aiming for the basket. The coach had no interest in me—as if I didn't even exist.

I changed again, this time trying volleyball—and the same thing happened. Only this time, it was much worse. I participated in a tournament against other schools and found myself on the bench. Since our team was winning by a pretty good margin—if I'm not mistaken, it was 12–0 with fifteen minutes left. My coach decided to give me a chance on the court. It was a fiasco. The players of the other team realized at once that I was the weak link and targeted all the balls to me. They almost managed to tie the game. Of course I didn't see the final whistle since the coach sent me back to my warm spot on the bench. My team won, nevertheless—and fortunately—and I decided volleyball wasn't my sport.

"Persistence always goes hand in hand with passion."

A little while later, a school friend invited me to visit a judo academy with him and I had the opportunity to watch training. The teacher asked if I wanted to participate.

I answered that I didn't have a uniform, but he said he would lend me one. When the class was over, he said I picked up the sport pretty well and if I wanted to continue training, I could be a great athlete.

I went home that day excited. For the first time, I had received a compliment through sport, an incentive to train, and an opportunity to become a real athlete. I had a purpose and a teacher who believed in me—and I couldn't disappoint him. The next day, I was already registered and ready to begin my new sport.

There were some quirks to learning judo that I could truly understand only some time afterward. For example, in a sport where the winner is the one who knocks the other down more times, the first lesson is how to fall. In my first month of classes, the only thing I really learned was how to fall down correctly without getting hurt. When we lose the fear of falling, only then do we start to train in the techniques that can help us take down adversary. With these lessons, we were taught that in the beginning, we would be falling much more than bringing down—and it was really like that. In the first few months, all of the academy members in my age group could throw me on the mat—no matter if I was heavier or stronger than some of them.

The most important thing, however, was that my teacher continued to believe in me and told me that if I kept training hard, I could be the state champion one day. That positive expectation somehow ignited a passion for judo inside of me, and persistence came with it. No matter how intense the training was, I didn't even consider quitting an option.

Today, I know how important it is to know how to lose so that you can become a champion. We can't let our losses bring us down. We know the losses will come, but we should stay above them and not let them shake our self-esteem and self-confidence. I'm certain of it: we learn more with our mistakes than when we get it right.

My teacher was right in what he told me in class that day. I became a champion, not only of my state but also of the north–northeast region—for four years in a row. The most important things were not the medals, however, but the lessons I learned during this time in my life. The most important aspect of all this was not the medals, but rather the learning experience of this stage in my life. For the first time, I pursued a goal, persevered in developing my skills, and knew that my success depended directly on my effort and persistence. In the end, all of my dedication was worth it.

After everything I just told you, I ask again: is it possible to develop persistence? With full conviction, I say yes. First, you have to have a goal because you can't be persistent without knowing where you're going or what you want to achieve. You absolutely should get to know people who go hiking or trekking. They go, step by step, until they reach their goal. Do you think it would be possible to persist throughout the journey without knowing your final destination—or even why you should go there in the first place? Of course not. You need to first determine your objective in order to achieve it.

Start trying to find something you like to do. Create small goals to achieve initially, celebrating each small victory and then progressively increasing the challenges as you move along. Whatever the task may be, you can always try to get better at it, with more focus and skill. We need to cherish every moment, appreciating it while still seeking a way to take another step forward in our life project. Don't forget! If we want to be recognized, we need to do the best we can now in order to cultivate persistence. It's like with whoever plants a tree. At the beginning of its life, the tree will need to be watered every day, but then it can survive by itself, and we can enjoy the shade and its fruits.

7 OPTIMISM,
OUR DRIVING FORCE

"Imagine a new story for your life and believe in it."

—Paulo Coelho, writer

We need to be optimistic! Everyone agrees we can live only in the present—the future is only an expectation. The past exists only in our memories: whether it's good or bad, we can't change it. We also know that today, we are a result of our past actions. Now comes the key question: how would you like to live the next few years of your life?

Can you visualize a good life? In good health? With money to do what you want to do? With a successful career and recognition? After all, if the future is an expectation, you need to learn to build images of success—in your mind at first. So where is your focus?

Let's imagine we're walking in a totally dark cave. No worries; we have a powerful flashlight that'll help us reach the exit. First, however, we need to get through this narrow path on the edge of a really deep cliff. In the beginning, we were standing on firm ground, walking on rocks. But now that we've reached this really high cliff, the only way to cross to the other side is through a narrow passage that is in complete darkness. Do we need to use the flashlight? Of course! Where should we focus our flashlight? On the straight and narrow passage, we're about to go through, or on the cliff?

The difference between the optimist and the pessimist is this: the pessimist will focus their flashlight on the cliff and may never make it across the narrow way. If you go through focusing on the cliff, you'll surely fall.

The optimist, on the other hand, although in the same dangerous situation, knows they should use their flashlight to focus on the path, exactly where they need to step, and will go slowly and carefully, one step at a time.

This analogy clearly shows the different modes of thinking of a pessimist and an optimist. The pessimist expects the worst and suffers through anticipation, projecting that fear inward and outward. He is used to living like this, anxious all the time, scared of losing the things he likes the most and thinking the world is against him. Not only that, but he also doesn't trust anyone and without a doubt is very close to becoming depressed.

The optimist tries to focus on solutions rather than problems. He always has a positive expectation regarding his future, which gives him an advantage of feeling good in the present and looking forward to a better tomorrow. This outlook increases his motivation and invigorates his internal strength.

Indeed, it is important to note that nobody becomes optimistic or pessimistic by chance. There are reasons behind such choices. Some argue that the environment influences us, while others say it's a matter of genetics. Some even claim that we acquire negative thinking habits. I won't delve deep into the causes, but as an amateur, I believe that everyone has a little bit of truth in what they say.

Imagine you raise two dogs of the same breed in your home. One of them is encouraged through good news, success stories, and positive messages. The other is fed negative stories of failure. When you go home every day, to which dog do you tell more stories from the outside world? Is the dog fed on pessimism now stronger than the dog fed on optimism? Now imagine these dogs are actually inside of you. To which one do you give more attention? Isn't it time to balance out the diets of these imaginary animals?

"After all, if the future is an expectation, you need to learn to build images of success—in your mind at first. So where is your focus?"

Did you ever think your pessimism could infect everyone living in your home? That your son could stop daring to dream, stop daring to have a better life because he believes he won't be able to reach his dreams? Have you thought about how many opportunities he lost because he didn't believe it would go right?

As a pessimist, you block your own development. Although the opportunities might be right in front of you, you still turn your face to see the difficulties. The pessimist is always saying it is very difficult to get a good job, to get married, to make money. In short, they'll say everything they'll ever want will be very difficult to get.

Many pessimists defend their points of view with strong arguments. To some extent, they're right because we see the world according to our beliefs. I propose changing the way we look at the facts because even though today might have been difficult, that doesn't mean tomorrow will be. Difficulties have to exist in our lives to help us grow and get stronger. We can't lose hope in the future just because our present isn't going so well. In the same way, we can't keep waiting for good things to happen in our life without doing our part.

We need to prepare—things don't just fall from the sky. We need to plant good seeds in the here and now so they can reap the fruits of success.

The optimist believes they can move forward in the direction of their dreams and have a certainty that their achievements will be there as a result of their efforts. They believe opportunities will appear in their life and that they will always be in the right place at the right time to take the chances life throws at them—every single day. Life is about choices. We can choose the best, be attentive to what happens around us, or choose what we want for our lives.

Let's imagine that we are a coach of a soccer team and our goal is to win the upcoming tournament. Before anything, we need to choose which athletes will be selected, what the criteria is for this selection, who would be better playing in the attack, in the defense, or in the midfield. Of course we will choose the best (in our opinion) because we want to win. In the game of life, we should be doing the same thing with our thoughts. If we want to win the game, we need optimistic thoughts as the players of our team so they can help us achieve personal success.

"We need to prepare—things don't just fall from the sky. We need to plant good seeds in the here and now so they can reap the fruits of success."

Optimistic thoughts can be powerful difference makers in our life. They make us believe in the possibility of victory, and with that thought we're more motivated to train, to concentrate our efforts, and to withstand and overcome losses. We realize the more diffi-cult the obstacle is, the more valuable the victory will be toward our desired dream to win in life. We have the power of choice. To be pessimistic or optimistic is a matter of personal choice; we decide how to think and how to react, and where we should focus our future expectations. The decision to be optimistic gives us the courage to go after our dreams.

Imagine you're heading to a meeting. Suddenly, you blow out a tire, and what follows? Your reaction. How are you going to react? Are you going to thank God for having gotten rid of something bad that might have happened if your tire didn't blow out? Or are you going to be furious and believe you lost an incredible opportunity because of a flat tire? You have the power to decide what to believe, but make sure you know your reaction will have an impact on your life. How many people who would do anything but be late have reached places where tragic events were happening and they were hit by stray bullets, or arrived right on time for a robbery and thought, "If my tire had blown out, I wouldn't be here right now?" or "If I had just lost my bus this morning…"

Sometimes, we don't even have a second to pass along information to help someone because we're always in a hurry solving our own problems. Reflect on the unpleasant and unexpected events in your life because most of the time, they are blessings in disguise that only optimists can see. We need to be attentive to simple examples from everyday life so we don't get upset over the little things. How many times have we lost control because a driver in front of us did something wrong, creating scary, mental blocks in our head where it could have ended in tragedy?

I propose a single day of absolute optimism. Let's try and change our negative habits—instead of hearing negative news on the radio in your car, listen to a motivational podcast or music that inspires something positive within you. Let's just—for a day—avoid getting into the negative area and unnecessary criticism. We can be more thankful and more supportive.

We should use those mental images to visualize a future when we've reached our dreams. Let's be optimistic so we can do more and more. Don't miss the opportunity to be optimistic—even if it's just for one day. Perhaps you like that attitude and want to repeat it on more and more days after today.

What I speak about optimism, I have observed throughout my life, with all the difficulties I have faced. I am certain that I only managed to overcome them because I was optimistic and believed that I would find a solution. I was sure that all I needed to do was to keep working and maintain a positive mindset, trusting that I would find a way out. And guess what? It actually worked for me!

I'm a person, not unlike so many others, with limitations and weaknesses, but even so, with optimism and the other skills addressed in this book, I was able to overcome a lot of difficult moments. I thought that with these stories, I could share my experiences of being optimistic through our social project at the Otacílio Gama Institute.

Would it be possible for those children to become more optimistic, even in their precarious situation, by having sports as an incentive? If they identify with the right sport, if they have the right coach to teach them and believe in them, and if they could keep training to hit all the small goals in their sports—would that be enough to help them become champion in their life?

Well, we could try. My first challenge was to find coaches committed to the same cause, who had the appropriate background to take on the task. They had to be more than just coaches—they had to be tutors and teachers who would invest in the personal development of these children. It took six months of hard work to find these teachers and the necessary resources so our dream of creating the Project Factory of Winners could kick off right.

With all the pieces in place, we began to try and shape children into more optimistic and hopeful people who believed in a better future and wanted it for themselves. Despite being just an amateur in the field of psychology, today, twenty and six years after I started this project and with all the results that have come through it, I am absolutely positive that it is possible to help others become more optimistic.

That's an interesting finding. Dr. Martin Seligman is indeed a renowned figure in the field of psychology, particularly for his work on positive psychology and optimism. In his book "The Optimistic Child" published in 2007, he concluded that teaching 10-year-old children the skill of thinking and acting with optimism reduces the likelihood of depression during adolescence.

Dr. Seligman's research aligns with the notion that optimism can be developed and cultivated, even in children. By providing them with the tools and strategies to approach life's challenges with a positive mindset, we can potentially enhance their well-being and resilience.

It's worth noting that optimism is not about denying or ignoring negative experiences but rather about facing them with a constructive and hopeful perspective. Teaching children to reframe situations, focus on strengths, and develop a belief in their ability to overcome difficulties can have long-lasting positive effects on their mental health and overall outlook on life.

In the book *Flourish: An Understanding of Happiness and Well-Being—and How to Achieve Them* (2011), Seligman gives us three aspects that make up the psychological well-being of individuals (or of interactions within a community): optimism, motivation, and resilience. Seligman, in the second part of *Flourish*, reflects on possible paths of personal growth, ways to improve positive emotion, and our base of self-actualization. These served as a reflection guide to putting these principles into practice at the Otacílio Gama Institute.

Seligman highlights an interesting point defining the entire purpose of the Institute: pessimistic people are more susceptible to becoming depressed than optimistic people. They also, overall, have lower performance in school, in sport, and at work, as well as being the more unstable one in a relationship. Seligman calls for further investigation into which factors influence the development of resilience and well-being, as well as community welfare—which we investigate in this book.

8 UNLEASHING THE POWER OF FAITH

"Faith is the path that leads us to the right to a second chance. Believe, believe in yourself and in God: this inner capacity to believe can motivate you to want better things for yourself and for the ones you love. With faith, everything fits."

—Abilio Diniz, Brazilian businessman

I believe that we possess a human body and a spirit, and just as we are connected to our mother through a physical umbilical cord at birth, we also have a similar spiritual umbilical cord connecting our spirit to a divine source. Unlike the physical umbilical cord that needs to be cut when we are born, the divine cord never breaks because through it, one day we will return to our source.

Believing we are connected to a higher power will be the biggest challenge in our lives. Finding that faith within us can help us overcome all obstacles we may go through in our lives. This magical force, powerful as it is, can break through all kinds of barriers, destroy all our enemies, face all our dangers and challenges, and extinguish our deepest fears. Faith is, without a doubt, the greatest of all the powers a human being can have. It can turn the impossible into something possible and lead the human being closer to God.

I believe we can look for ways to enhance our communication with God through this divine cord. To do that, we need to first believe in the perception that it exists. The more aware we are of our connection with God, the stronger and more radiant the channel becomes that carries our faith. This divine energy duct should be used throughout our entire lives; it connects us with our Creator's source.

I believe when we communicate with God, the flow of energy that comes through our cord makes us much more powerful, creative, and optimistic. We feel like we're really connected with God and filled with love and faith. There are people who do not believe in the existence of this cord, but regardless, it exists, remaining static without any flow, until the time comes when it will be used solely as a channel for returning to its source..

Can you believe you are closely connected to God? If you are connected with your divine force, who will be able to harm you? Try to visualize your divine channel as a bright golden conduit, feel the energy that you will generate by using your mind to access your core strength. Believe! Faith is within yourself, and the more you believe, the stronger it becomes.

I'd like to propose a challenge to you, my reader. Let's begin visualizing our connection cord and, twice a day, let's communicate, according to each individual's religion and principles, with our Higher Power. Rest assured that each contact you make will serve to increase your faith, leaving you feeling more protected and secure.

Faith is born inside of each one of us, so we have to go look for it within our deepest selves, to awaken this force that is asleep and unlimited, just waiting to be discovered. Believe we have this power and we can channel this connection with God to become stronger to withstand any challenge life throws at us. I believe that faith is the most precious gift that the Creator has bestowed upon us, and to abandon this power throughout life's journey is to relinquish the most important tool for building our personal success, happiness, and well-being.

There is a fable that I particularly like. A father gave his son a box as a gift and told him that inside it contained everything, he needed to be happy. Within it were all the riches, talents, health, and ultimately, all the power and fulfillment a person could desire. The son only needed to learn how to open the box to not lose anything that was inside. The son then asked, "With what kind of tool will I open the box?" The father replied, "With faith, my child."

Indeed, it would be a great waste to go through life without even attempting to open the greatest gift we received from our Creator. By sharing this fable, my purpose is for us to recognize that we have this magical box and then work towards discovering the secret to open it.

 If we open this box at least once, it would make it easier to open it hundreds of more times thereafter. We have to try, every day, until we're successful.

Our Father has given us this magnificent gift because he believes that one day, we will be able to fully open our box of faith and thus help transform humanity.

We should always keep in mind that faith is not instantaneous. It develops slowly, through actions. Our faith is unique. No two people in the world have the same faith; it is individual. Don't expect others to have the same faith as you. Everyone has his or her own.

Remember what you do is much more important than what you say. You should always live in accordance with your faith. Believe in love, believe in goodness, believe in life, believe you can go further, believe you can be healthier, believe you can have more money, believe you can have a good career, believe you can have a wonderful family and amazing friends. Believe you are a child of God and He will never cut your umbilical cord.

"Believe! Faith is within you; the more you believe, the stronger it will become."

9 RESILIENCE:
THE SHIELD OF CHAMPIONS

"Our minds influence the key activity of the brain, which then influences everything: perception, cognition, thoughts and feelings, personal relationships—they're all a projection of you."

—Deepak Chopra, doctor and writer

Life is always telling us we need to be resilient. Getting out of our comfort zone will be a constant in our existence. We cannot be slaughtered by adversities from our everyday lives. Babies, before they're born, enjoy the comforts of their mother's womb. We're fed through the umbilical cord. We don't feel cold or heat. Everything is perfect, until the day comes when we're born into this world and our comfort zone disappears. From then on, we have to keep adapting to every new stage in life.

As I mentioned in the previous chapters, we need to learn how to fall in order to learn how to rise up again. This has to do with resilience. I want to show in a practical way that we need to search for the characteristics within us that will help us win in life.

Resilience is one of those fundamental skills that are crucial for human development. Nature itself provides several examples that inspire us to develop this ability. We need to learn to live with climate change and the change of the seasons. Look at how animals can survive despite being targeted by predators. These are small examples among multitudes of others that present themselves every single day.

We human beings need to learn to live with difficulties, look for our inner balance, and know how we should react to these difficulties. This will be decisive for our future. Difficulties and problems will always exist, but with every problem, try your best to react with resilience, take a proactive attitude, and always head into the direction of your larger goal. We cannot despair in difficult situations. Our growth limit is proportional to our capacity for resilience. When all seems lost, a way will always appear—with others who are resilient already on its path.

"Being resilient is different from being tough. You can bend, but don't break. It's not swimming against the current but using it to get out of the water."

There is a legend in judo books that tells the story of Master Jigoro Kano, the creator of this martial art. It is said that he would spend hours observing the snow falling on trees and noticed that some very strong branches would accumulate a large amount of snow and eventually break, while the willow tree, with its long and slender branches, would receive a certain amount of snow and bend under the weight, but gradually return to its original position once all the snow had fallen. Through his observations, he developed judo, whose principle is seemingly to yield and then counterattack.

Remember: Being resilient is different from being resistant. You may bend, but you won't break It's not about swimming against the current, but rather using it to get out of the water.

Here is another fable I once read and found very interesting: It tells the story of a horse that fell into a dry well, and the strongest young people from the village were called upon to tie a rope and pull the horse out. Despite using all their strength, they couldn't rescue the horse as it was too heavy. When the horse owner was desperate and didn't know what to do, an old man who lived in the mountains appeared. Observing the situation, the elderly man asked if they had tools like a shovel. Even though the villagers didn't understand why the old man wanted a shovel, they fetched what he asked for. The old man then said, "Start digging the soil and throw it into the well." As the villagers threw soil onto the horse, it shook its body and stood on the accumulating soil until the well was filled, allowing the horse to escape.

This story gives a metaphor for our difficulties. We should be resilient to overcome challenges and believe the more they appear in our lives, the more we grow, and every problem can give us a way out.

I have an interesting story of something that happened to me that shows the importance of resilience. I had just turned eighteen and was serving in the Brazilian army, running on pure satisfaction of just completing the first week of the Army Officer Course. I was an athlete used to hard, physical training, but we had started training in unity, which was very tiring.

We spent hours learning how to march and how to follow commands. At that time, my colleagues and I didn't have the slightest idea that we were being evaluated on certain criteria, like physical activity, behavior, discipline, and emotional balance, on top of our curricular studies. I couldn't have imagined that, on that first Friday, I would hear shouting from right next to me, "Gama!!! dumb!!! Get the march right!!" After that first scolding, however, it was nearly impossible to get anything right.

The screaming continued, one scream after another; the screams were getting louder and louder and I couldn't get the march right. After a lot of yelling came the verdict: "You're confined to the barracks for the entire weekend!" I felt extremely wronged. It was my first week in the army and I was the first one to be punished and detained. I had spent the entire week training, trying to do my best, and at the end, I was called stupid and incompetent and punished! If I had known at that moment that it was nothing personal and was just a part of training, it would have been much easier.

The major in command wanted to gauge my reaction over the next few days and see how I handled the pressure. I spent the weekend alone at the barracks. While I was brooding over my anger, I remembered a book I had read that spoke about the power of thought. It had said that if we kept a thought of anger against any person, this same kind of thinking would come back in our direction. The best way to stop this negative cycle in its tracks was to make a mental effort to find out what the other person found positive in this situation and try to understand it.

I took a deep breath and began to put those teachings into practice. I took the feelings of injustice out from my thoughts and my feelings of internal revolution went away with it. In silence, I started to think about positive images.

A few days later, I had the chance to apply for the position of social director for the Student Union of the 15th Infantry Battalion. I was elected because I had demonstrated my willingness to contribute and work towards the goals of my class. As I started thinking differently, the commanding officer's attitude towards me changed. I could sense that he genuinely liked me and I no longer felt threatened or unsafe in that environment.

I observed that he was treating other people in my class the same way he treated me. Every two weeks, he would focus his attention on a different person. I came to realize that it wasn't actually persecution but rather a method to assess everyone's mental and emotional resilience.

Today, we see bright and intelligent young people who cannot accept the word no or a critique of their performance, who get upset and lose opportunities to reach the highest levels of their profession because they don't know how to be resilient or humble themselves to listen to some advice.

I placed this chapter of resilience right after the chapters on optimism and faith because I think they are both fundamental for personal development and success in any area of your life. We all need to delve deep within ourselves to nurture and refine these qualities. Resilience serves as our driving force to rise again. It must reach out to its siblings—faith and optimism—as they walk hand in hand. They need to be united in the task of strengthening us to overcome all obstacles and challenges in order to achieve personal success, wealth, and happiness.

10 THE MIRROR OF SELF-ESTEEM

*"A big mistake: to believe oneself to be more important
than one is and to underestimate oneself from what
one is worth."*

—Johann Wolfgang von Goethe, writer

Start right now to search for something positive within yourself,
don't fall into the trap of self-depreciation. Nobody is completely
bad, find what you have best and strengthen that aspect. Suppress
the worst in you, try to connect with real-life or fictional people who
possess qualities that you admire.

Create a positive self-image, try and emulate a character with
these qualities you want, and you'll be astounded how they'll emerge
inside of you. If you can believe that you can add these new values within yourself, your subconscious will proceed to make the
change naturally.

Be certain that the more you can love yourself, the more others
will also like you. Remember that you are like a precious gem: the
more you are polished with good qualities, the more people can see
your shine.

As mentioned in previous chapters, you are writing your own story every day, and in that story, you are both the hero and the main character. Don't let others define who you are or how far you can go. That responsibility belongs solely to you.

When we strengthen our self-esteem, we can also develop a greater appreciation for the people we interact with. We can avoid unnecessary criticism and complaints and live with more intensity and love.

In the Bible, one of the commandments says, "Love God above all things and love thy neighbor as thyself." We have free will to make our own decisions and choices.

We need to be ethical and treat others as we would like to be treated ourselves. One of the biggest reasons for fights and wars is the fact that people don't want to receive what they are giving out. When they are giving rudeness out, they want to receive affection; when they are giving acidic criticism out, they want to be applauded. I'll leave you with a question here: What are you giving to the people you love? The time has come to make a revolution inside of you and change personal paradigms. Stop and look at how and what you're doing.

Start today—build your success model. It is essential that the construction has a solid base of support so it can reach higher heights. This base will be the love you have for yourself.

That's a great analogy! Building self-esteem is indeed a process that requires a solid foundation. Just like constructing a house, we need high-quality materials for the foundation, and in this case, respect serves as a solid base. Respecting others and expecting the same in return is crucial. It promotes healthy boundaries and creates a positive environment where mutual respect can thrive. By treating others with respect and demanding respect for ourselves, we contribute to the development of healthy self-esteem.

In the next stage of construction, we will use bricks to build the walls of the house. These bricks need to be sturdy to withstand the criticisms and trivialities of social relationships. They should be coated with the mortar of wisdom and humility to strengthen the structure of the house. Then we will cover our house with the tiles of dignity.

We can only give to others what we carry within ourselves. Love for others will only be possible if we love ourselves.

"Remember you are like a precious gemstone: the more you're cut with good qualities, the more people will witness your brilliant shine."

11 SELF-CONFIDENCE: LIFE'S ENGINE

"If you have confidence in yourself, you can have confidence in me, you can have confidence in people, you can have confidence in existence."

—Osho, spiritual leader

Developing self-confidence holds great significance in our lives and how we interact with the world. In order to grow, whether it be in our professional lives or relationships, earning the trust and confidence of others is crucial. It is difficult to thrive in any aspect of life without being seen as dependable. Initially, we must have faith in ourselves to gain the trust of others. If we don't trust ourselves, how can we expect others to trust us?

Trust is one of the qualities that we instinctively observe in people. From the moment we are born, we can sense it in our mother's eyes and feel the comfort and safety in her arms. There is a profound certainty that she will fulfill our needs and take care of us. The need for trust remains with us throughout our entire lives. It is no wonder that individuals seek relationships with those who provide them with a sense of security. The presence of trust, both in trusting others and being trusted ourselves, can significantly influence our success or failure in life.

The foundation of any relationship, whether personal or professional, always relies on confidence and trust. No one feels at ease living or working with someone they cannot trust. We place our trust in people, institutions, projects, and narratives. Trust plays a crucial role in the economy as well, as anything that holds significance must be trustworthy, or else it loses its value.

You may wonder why I am discussing trust and confidence when this chapter focuses on self-confidence. The reason is that when we have faith in others and feel their confidence in us, we learn how to cultivate our own self-confidence. Therefore, it is essential to trust our children every day, starting with small dosages, by giving them simple tasks to help them achieve small goals at home, in school, and in extracurricular activities like sports or art.

We are also born with the innate capacity for trust, but, unfortunately, when we are children, adults love us with excessive protection, which can turn us into insecure people who don't know how to trust in ourselves. How does that happen? Normally, we try to protect our children from something we believe to be dangerous or unpleasant. If a child climbs up a wall, for example, the vast majority of parents or grandparents will shout, "Don't go up there; you're going to fall and get hurt!" Or they might say, "Don't run or you'll fall!" The right thing to do would be to instead approach them, let the child face that challenge themselves and be attentive to catch them if he or she falls.

We also shouldn't let a child lose confidence in themselves by being overzealous because this might stop them from daring to do something different and have a very negative impact on their development. That's why we see so many smart people and great students who don't become good professionals—because they don't believe in themselves.

I would like parents to read this chapter carefully because the skill of self-confidence in their children will depend a lot on the attitudes of their family. Children need to understand that the adults have confidence in them.

"The support base of any relationship, be it personal or professional, will always be confidence and trust."

Scolding children when they say something silly in front of visitors might make them fear speaking in the future, for fear of punishment. We, as parents, are building a personality in people to win in life, and they need to be confident in themselves to do it. I observed that children in our social project who, perhaps because they're not subjected to excessive protection, were more self-confident than other children, and they had more grit and determination for sports, for competitions, and for life.

I'm going to illustrate what I said by telling you about something that happened to me and my son. Othon was a very spoiled boy—super-protected at home by his family members and by the staff at the house. Perhaps that was why at eight years old, he still cried every day when he had to go to school. He also cried throughout and stopped only when he could go home. Several times a week, he was called in to talk with a psychologist at Marista School.

Realizing this weakness, I understood that at home, it would be harder to help, so I decided to put my lesson into practice at the

Institute. I asked for the teachers to treat him like any other student, with none of the privileges of being my son.

In the beginning, I placed him to practice judo, but I left it at that since I wanted to let him choose a different sport if he wanted to. After two months at judo, Othon asked to change to basketball, a sport that would soon become his passion. On the court, he learned how to work on a team, interacting with children from a social reality very different from his, who were more confident. He started to reach small developmental goals, like improving his tackling or dribbling. As his passion for the sport flourished, Othon started to develop persistence when trying to improve his performance and finally discovered that the only way to get better in his skill was through his own effort.

As his skill increased, his self-confidence and self-esteem also grew. After a little while training at the Institute, he started to train on a team at Marista School and went on to participate in student championships.

The most important part of all this was that my insecure boy had transformed into a self-confident, determined, and focused teenager. The powers of self-confidence and courage he acquired through the practice of sports were—without a doubt—very important in his development into the writer and speaker he is today, who has spoken in front of audiences to thousands of people.

The seeds of trust need to be sown. Only then—as a real seed—can trust grow out of the ground. Slowly, the seed will begin developing over time and then will make itself known and seen by others. When confident people form institutions, these are the ones we trust the most.

Working on self-confidence is undoubtedly a challenge in our own personal development. By incorporating the qualities mentioned earlier in this book, we can infuse confidence into our actions and bring about transformative changes in our lives. By doing so, we can overcome obstacles with success and turn our dreams into reality.

Furthermore, this narrative shows us the importance of self-confidence and illustrates how nurturing it can result in personal growth, success, and the realization of our aspirations.

12 SOLIDARITY:
A BLESSING FOR HUMANITY

"Solidarity is not just an act of charity; it is an attitude that recognizes the interdependence of all human beings and seeks to promote collective well-being."

— Dalai Lama

By helping others and engaging in good deeds enables us to develop an incredible power. Just like the law of gravity, this power works its magic. It doesn't matter whether you believe in gravity or not; it remains a universal force and deserves our respect. There's no point in thinking you can jump from a high point and not fall because gravity will inevitably pull you back down.

This principle also applies to the law of solidarity. If you assist someone who hasn't achieved their goals, don't expect immediate gratitude, as someone else will eventually help you. This law is unchangeable. Whatever kindness we sow here, we will reap in return.

Scientific research now proves that helping others is one of the sources of lasting satisfaction in our lives. When we establish a habit of selflessly assisting others without expecting anything in return, we experience a profound sense of well-being.

Some individuals spend their entire lives expecting help but aren't willing to help anyone themselves. They rely on coworkers, teachers, and family members while constantly waiting for assistance. Sometimes, they even become resentful when things don't go as planned. What they fail to realize is that the moment they change their behavior and begin selflessly helping others, they will witness transformative changes in their own lives. Their perspective of the world will be radically different. They will also understand that there are people out there who are willing to offer help without any expectations, and this realization will contribute to their personal growth. So I ask you: How much are you willing to help others without waiting for any form of appreciation?"

When I mention "doing good," it's important to understand that it's not limited to those who have a high financial status. Anyone who desires to engage in acts of kindness has numerous opportunities to do so in their lives. Treating people with respect and consideration is a way to do good, as everyone appreciates being treated well and respected. Even something as simple as opening the window of your car to accept an advertisement someone is handing out can be a form of assistance.

We can create our "kindness journal" to daily jot down the number of people we had the opportunity to do a favor for. If you are aware that this is important for your personal growth, you will remember to do it.

We need to be attentive to the opportunities we have to help people. They will appear at all times, in the form of advice, incentive, a handshake, a look of approval, letting someone pass you on the road, a good shoulder to cry on, supporting a cause, etc. We can contribute in many different ways. We need to cultivate within ourselves the quality of being sympathetic to people because this will make a huge difference in our future—believe me! This decision could have a powerful impact on personal development and help us develop all the other qualities contained in this book. Practice the art of doing good and you'll turn into a more spiritually developed and happier person.

"When we create the habit of helping others without expecting anything in return, we will feel happier."

If you really want to help someone, the first step is to trust them. Believing in people, betting on their potential, has an amazing effect on human development in the same way it had a positive effect on my life and in the lives of the students at the Otacílio Gama Institute. And it can also transform the lives of those you believe in.

In previous chapters, I talked about how I became a judo athlete and how this sport influenced my life. All of it came about because of the attitude and mindset of my coach, who believed I could be a great athlete.

I also talked about memories from my childhood, that my father believed in children on the street and how this was important in changing their lives too. The trust and respect, deposited in forms of job opportunities, advice, and motivation, created positive attitudes that helped their personal development.

Today, I can say with absolute conviction that after twenty and six years, the Otacílio Gama Institute—which served as the transforming element in the lives of our students—succeeded in making its students believe they could be champions in life.

If you want to really help people, believe in them. A lot of those times, you might be disappointed; however, when you get it right, your satisfaction will supersede any and all disappointments. There are plenty of opportunities to help people, whether it's at home, in the neighborhood, uptown, in your own city, or in the world. Anywhere, we can always be more supportive and do good. Believe it! By doing so, you will become happier and more empowered.

"Make the decision now to help people and do good. This will change your life."

CONCLUSION

We are starting a journey—of no return—to the future. We need to be prepared to accomplish all of our dreams, to secure our spot in the winners' gallery with others who are successful in their businesses, family, and relationships. To embark on this trip, we need to seek within ourselves the basic skills to make the most of the opportunities we have in front of us and deal with the difficulties the certainly will emerge.

The skills discussed in this book are nothing new to anyone; everyone's heard of them before. Everyone can have them to a greater or lesser extent. They are not magical, but they can produce miracles in people's lives. These skills will be responsible for all the decisions we'll make from here on out, as they once were for all the decisions we made in the past.

What I propose on this journey into the future is to reflect and evaluate, with our own conscience, the advantages of taking over the making of a prosperous, happy, and healthy future for ourselves—and for the people we love. Our journey starts now. Put OPTIMISM and FAITH in your metaphorical luggage —they are skills that will help you write your script. If you dream big and believe you can achieve your dreams, this will be a determining factor for your life. You need to be willing to pay the price. You cannot forget to have COURAGE to dare in the most difficult moments. But you also need FAITH to support your OPTIMISM, which will uphold your COURAGE.

Remember, however, that our plans must be matured and sometimes it takes time to achieve your bolder goals to be achieved. In these cases, you will need to take PERSISTENCE along with you. We cannot give up on our dreams—we need to persist. Forces above our understanding operate in nature and help us at all times. We need to continue persisting and the universe will conspire in our favor. Learn to like what you do or ask God to show you a decent job in which you can help people and earn the money that will make you happy.

Don't forget to pack your GOODWILL because it will help you open the most difficult doors and create groups to work in tune with you.

Remember quitting is not an option; for our trip into the future, we need to be prepared to face a lot of difficulties and we need RESILIENCE—one of the skills that makes winners. Winners also lose, but they're not defeated; they continue forward on their search for success and go on until they find it. Don't forget that on our journey to the future, all relationships and activities will depend on trust and confidence.

We can't be at peace when we are forced to live with people or with institutions we don't trust, which is why it is essential to take our SELF-CONFIDENCE with us for the future. This skill gives others confidence in us. When we have self-confidence, we have a powerful component to pack away for our trip to the future, with the possibility to create the basis of trust in ourselves to find success.

If you want to be happy on your trip to the future, don't forget to take SELF-ESTEEM, and learn to love yourself. This is a *must* for anyone who wishes to be successful. If you don't like yourself, you will not be able to like anyone else. We need to generate the love within ourselves to be able to expand it to others.

No wonder that this is the first commandment: "Love God above all things and love thy neighbor as thyself."

If you're taking your self-esteem on your trip, you'll also need SOLIDARITY, and with this magical power, you can look at the world in a different way. Your success will then be complete.

Remember that on the trip to the future, these things will be with you, as well as all the people you love and all the opportunities you desire. Go forward, go prepared, and don't look back! Have a safe trip.

YOUR SKILLS NOTEBOOK

The other day, while reviewing my notes, I read some of the aspirations I had as a young dreamer. While reading them, I found that a lot of what I wanted to accomplish was there, written by me, as if it was a prediction. There was will and trust in my writing that it would happen. Today, I challenge you to do the same. Put your dream on paper. The universe may like the idea and sign a contract with you.

What are the nine skills you think you already have? Do you remember what they are? Goodwill, courage, persistence, optimism, faith, resilience, self-esteem, self-confidence, and solidarity.

_____

_____

_____

_____

_____

_____

Which skills do you need to grow?

_____

_____

_____

_____

_____

_____

What is your biggest dream?

_____

_____

_____

_____

_____

What have you done to improve your natural talents and transform them into skills that can make you stand out?

_____

_____

_____

_____

_____

What have you done to turn your skills into excellence?

_____

_____

_____

_____

_____

Are you ready, with energy and faith, to work on these necessary changes in your life?

_____

_____

_____

_____

_____

_____

ABOUT THE AUTHOR

Othamar Gama is the founder and former CEO of the Faculty of Medical Sciences of Paraiba, creator and president of Intermares Hall convention Center in Brazil, founder and sponsor of the Otacílio Gama institute, developer of the Project of the First Job Opportunity initiative for youths from third-sector institution Otacílio Gama Institute, and the mastermind behind the Winner Factory project. He earned his master's degree in general business from ISCTE – Lisbon University Institute- and has bountiful experience as an entrepreneur in diverse fields such as education, construction, and advertising. Prior to becoming a prosperous businessman, he graduated with a bachelor's degree in civil engineering.

Moreover, Othamar has over 26 years of experience with third sector as president and sponsor of the Otacilio Gama Foundation, which has made a substantial difference in the lives of thousands of children from disadvantaged communities in Brazil. Through its remarkable work, the foundation provides invaluable support and assistance to those in need.

Othamar is a motivational speaker and researcher in self-development and positive psychology. This book, known as the "A Formula dos Vencedores," was written in Brazil and was hailed as a bestseller by Gente Publishers.

Othamar lives in Florida with his daughters, his wife. In addition to grasping hold of every moment spent with his family, he enjoys fighting judo, playing tennis, and is very passionate about gemstones - one of his hobbies is to go to his mine in Brazil to prospect Paraiba Tourmaline.